Soil, Seeds, Sun and Rain!
How Nature Works on a Farm!
Farming for Kids
Children's Agriculture Books

BABY PROFESSOR

EDUCATION KIDS

A farm is land used to grow plants and raise animals.

Farming is important because everyone needs food.

A farm
produces
all kinds of
plants and
animals that
people eat.

Ancient American families lived on a small farm raising almost everything they ate.

Today, there are fewer farms in the US than there were in the 1900's, but farmers today produce more.

Scientific methods and labor-saving machines increase farming production.

Plant varieties and fertilizers help to increase the yields of crops.

Farmers of livestock work throughout the year to take care of their animals.

Weather is extremely important for farmers.

Farmers must know the weather forecast for the coming months.

Without enough water, farm plants and animals may die.

If it rains too much, plants can die from drowning.

Too much heat will dry the farm leaving plants to die.

Farmers spend a lot of money on labor, seeds and equipment, so they have to know the most recent weather prediction.

Farmers base what they plant each year on the soil quality and weather predictions.

Farmers today use irrigation methods (sprinkler systems) to water crops.

Today's farmer is not just an agriculture expert but they also need to be a successful businessman, too.

QUICK FACT:

Agriculture is
the science
of farming.

There is so much more to know about farming. Research and have fun!

Visit

www.BabyProfessorBooks.com
to download Free Baby Professor eBooks
and view our catalog of new and exciting
Children's Books

Made in the USA
Columbia, SC
24 March 2021